Charley's
20/20 Visions

By: Charley Williams

Spiritually Inspired Mental Insights

CONTENTS

CONTENTS (continued)

CHARLEY

Charley. Charley. I asked of myself.
What will you do with this life you have left?
I set myself down to contemplate.
I'll make up my mind before it's too late.
So I then sought, the heavenly host.
Thru fervent prayer, I received the Holy Ghost.
The Holy Ghost purged, depths of my soul.
And life's mysteries began to unfold.
So.
I choose, the ultimate sacrifice.
The sacrifice which holds eternal life.
I must flee from the torments of hell.
And offer to help all mankind as well.
For this time on earth, it will soon pass.
But the torment of hell, will last, and last and …..

MY SOUL

The Soul, the conscience in man.
My soul, is conscious of man.
Till my soul shall find relief,
My soul is forever grieved.
Toil and strife did vex my soul.
Till conscious reign o'er my soul.
My soul yearns for inner peace.
Yet, conscious hiss, veiled deceits.
I'll raise the veil o'er my soul,
and rid inimical foes.
Oh to taste sweet liberty,
when my soul's conscience is free.

TIME

Time passes, as the sieving sand flows.
The mind reflects, precious scenes unfold.
Scenes balm and revive the weary soul.
This too shall pass, as gentle winds blow.

ACKNOWLEDGEMENT

I awoke this morning, to manna from heaven;
to essence of life, and carnal protection.

While I was deep in slumber of unconscious sleep;
Thy restrained my enemies, camped around me.

Neither attained by merits or feats of my own;
I reap all the blessings of this promised home.

When expending my all to do my very best;
thy suffer the shame of my unfaithfulness.

I've wondered through foreign lands of life's wilderness.
Seeking for my Soul's eternal home of rest.

And there is no other consoling peace I've found;
than when my faith's anchored, on thy holy ground.

Hoping to resist allures, into foreign lands;
less I'm found wondering, all over again.

HUMAN DOMINION

In the beginning, God created, Heavens and the earth.
And gives humans dominion, over the created work.
Thus, commences the legacy of human dominion;
over a Divine creation, by a freewill human.
Humans must devise means to survive on earth, in the flesh.
All carnal, social, and spiritual needs, must be addressed.
To perpetuate the carnal existence of humans,
heterosexuals lust for sexual interactions.
To nurture the human flesh, with essential provisions,
the earth supplies sustenance, as the Garden of Eden.
As procreation thrives, family systems are devised.
And, an order for rearing human offspring is prescribed.
As supplies of nurturing resources becomes finite,
the human inhabitation of the earth now takes flight.
Over mountains, down valleys, and across seas, humans roam.
Distance, time and place, forbids humans to return back home.
As families colonize, great civilizations form,
where essential needs for human survival are performed.
As human civilizations thrive, then, metastasize,
chaos arise, and threatens humans' future to survive.
Through passage of time, by products of creative minds,
a gradual reunion takes place, of all humankind.
Though, we are flesh, and warm blood runs in all human veins,
once family members proclaim, we're no longer the same.
Then pride-prejudice-patriotism seems to prevail,
The tenet to show love; towards all humankind, is dispelled.
The quest for one-humankind superiority reigns.
And it seems, that peace on earth, can no longer be attained.
Aggressive actions to conquer and annex is the quest.

Human slaughter, world disorder, at one human's behest.
What laps in time, did divinely created humankind,
have dominion, absent of, the spirit of the Divine?

MARRIAGE – ALWAYS IN SEASON

As the chill of night embraces the warmth of dawn;
A betrothal warmth's unions as the rising sun.

As the spring solstice revives a slumbering nature;
A faithful union excites sensual pleasures.

As earth bears sustenance from sunrays in summer;
A holy union begets our sons and daughters.

As falling leaves denotes its harvest time in fall;
Toils of unified endeavors yields blessed windfalls.

As winter cast its debilitating shadow:
Unfaithful unions dashes hopes of tomorrow.

The Kindred Spirit which binds loving helpmates;
Shall calm feeble minds as we contemplate our fates.

Marriage—A Terrible Thing to Waste.

SENSE-LESS

I've been non-sensed.
An inevitable consequence
of non-sensing times.

My friend once felt a physical pain.
Cringing I sensed, I'd endured the same.
A feeling I did sense.

My friend suffered emotional grief.
Impassioned I chide, a state too weak.
A feeling I didn't sense.

My friend once saw a beautiful thing,
A sight I sensed, the best ever seen.
A sight I did sense.

My friend envisioned a goal, but failed.
I fail to sense the depths of peril.
A sight I didn't sense.

My friend served a sumptuous table.
My taste buds senses were enabled.
A taste I did sense.

My friend once fell upon hungered times.
Yet, my appetite had no decline.
A taste I didn't sense.

My friend once sang a beautiful song.
My hearing it calmed my mental qualms.
A sound I did sense.

My friend cried out in mental anguish.
My hearing him sensed social faintness.
A sound I didn't sense.

My friend must sense it quite uncommon,
for me to sense another's problem.
I sense...I'm sense-less.

THE FAMILY VISION

Keep the family vision alive;
is the charge which we must abide.
Our elders taught that if we do,
blessings shall be bestowed on you.
Commence pursuit while still a youth.
Start by acknowledging life's truths.
First resolve that you will grow old,
so assure you have saved your soul.
Equip yourself for changing times,
Study; Aspire for a prepared mind.
Carnal desires aren't illusions;
so calm them through holy unions.
And if you're blessed to conceive,
nurture children for future needs.
Do your part to save the land,
stand up man; and take a firm stand.
To attain desires of your heart,
seek to be gainfully employed.
For if we seek the elder's plea,
we'll have family unity.

SEARCH FOR TOMORROW

The search for tomorrow is on everyone's mind.
Hoping that tomorrow will bring better times.
Knowing that yesterday is a thing of the past.
Maybe tomorrow is our day at last.
Searching for tomorrow is the thing of today.
It aids in the struggle to help time get away.
Our struggle gets greater as the time moves on.
Search for someone we can call our own.
Who brings tomorrow in such mysterious ways?
Does he know that tomorrow becomes today.
Tomorrow is known as the world's greatest excuse.
We put off today's work for tomorrow's use.

MILLENNIUMMAN

Have you taken time lately, to think about,
what will shortly come about?
A significant age is at hand,
the crowning of the next Millenniumman.

Here we stand in 1999, poised to cross
the millennium bridge of time.

Millenniumman, man of ages,
what shall scribes record on your span of pages?

Your counterpart, once apart,
had few technologies but did know God.

Your counterpart, twice apart,
was the beloved savor, the son of God.

Millenniumman, how shall you stand,
the inevitable focus on your lifespan?

How shall you be defined,
when scribes reflect you, as mankind?

Reflecting your godliness, humanity,
your love, morality, civility, your prosperity,
resourcefulness, dignity, your you, as mankind?

Millenniumman, will scribes surmise,
that you feared God and grew to be wise?

The Millenniumman bridge parts past from new.
Your past is written, your future is you.

Whether you dwell on failures,
or boast your success, It's up to you,
millennium anew.

Millenniumman, will you stand,
for the word of God,
in the new millennium land?

Millenniumman, stand.
If you fear God and plan to keep his commands.
Can we as man defend an honorable comparison,
to other Millenniummen?

Millenniumman, just wave your hand,
if you now plan to be a "God sent" man.

Raise your hand, if you now plan,
to read the word and let your voice be heard.

THE LOST FAMILY

By Divine Grace, an intriguing being catches one's eye.
A lure is cast, in hopes of a receptive reply.
The spirit erupts with joy, as the lure is warmly received.
Two loving souls embrace, and family is conceived.

As two hopes, two dreams, becomes one, matrimony hastens.
And unto this union, children are prized possessions.
Children are nurtured in wholesome family traditions;
because family is the essence of life's passions.

And lo, thru passage of time, the family nest empties.
Now, one hope, one dream, desires extended families.
As grace provides, the families extend, disburse and thrive.
Now, one hope, one dream, ponders; will our union survive?

So, the family devises plans, to meet from time to time.
Yet, over time, reunion requests starts to decline.
As the tree of life sheds the patriarch and matriarch,
desires to unite subsides, reunions fall apart.

Family communication portals, began to fail.
Desires of the one hope, one dream, no longer prevails.
Failure to reunite, abandons life's sacred treasure.
Cuddling of kindred spirits, is beyond measure.

Proverbially, the family forgot their way home.
And ultimately, became the clan of the unknowns.
Woe to family members who disconnect and scatter,
Cutting umbilical cords of family matters.

Patriarchs, protect your family from disengagements.
Matriarchs, nurture children in wholesome engagements.
May the family reunion, serve as the cornerstone,
helping lost family members, find their way back home.

THINK DON'T TRIP

Most humans today, live their lives in the strangest way.
We gaze in space only to find the factious life of cloud nine.
We don't really know what we want.
We speak peace and love, but really we don't.
Our reputations say we live a masquerade,
by progressing from mistakes our friends have made.
Let's open our minds to the facts of life.
Am I asking so great a sacrifice?
Think you fool, time for tripping is gone.
It's time to enjoy your earthly home.
If we would learn to think instead of trip;
and would use our minds instead of our lips;
our knowledge would grow our pockets would fill,
and we wouldn't have to worry about tomorrows meal.
If we would only think, instead of trip,
we would progress to the point our minds would flip.
But thinking is taboo for our carnal minds.
Understanding reality takes too much time.
Trip no longer, for it's impossible to know,
when the Lord shall come or we shall go.

RULES OF UNITY

Yes, I know we argue, fuss and fight,
but only for things we feel are right.
Can't you understand, that's how it's supposed to be,
so we may love each other tenderly.
No two people's minds are the same.
Maybe that's the reason we were given different names.
Conflicts and confusion will always arise.
So don't let them take you by surprise.
Cope with your problems each day of your life.
But learn just how much you should sacrifice.
Things will work out, oh yes they will.
You will learn that life is really a thrill.
Learn to love just being yourself,
but don't throw your problems on a mental shelf.
This will cause you to worry and feel uneased,
and you can no longer keep your partner pleased.
Follow the very first rule of the land.
Love and respect thy fellow man.

THE U.S. MIND

Why do we think the way we do?
We love someone we don't need to.
We care for someone no good for us.
We give to them all honor and trust.
But do they care for what we do?
To another they will always be true.

Why do we think the way we do?
We value all things we don't need to.

We need a bad ride to show downtown.
When the ride's down we're just another clown.
We got to have a hat with a suit to match.
Styles change so fast you can't keep up jack.

Why do we think the way we do?
Examples will tell what's right for you.
The fad we choose is not always good.
Examples will tell if we should.
I ask the question the whole day through,
Why do we think the way we do?

WHY DID I LET YOU GO?

Why did I let you go?
Even though I love you so.
I love you more than words can say.
Your love is the light that brightens my day.
You, my love, is the lady of my life.
How could I choose another for my wife?
Why did I let you go?
Even though I love you so.
Please return your love to me.
I was blind and could not see.
You were the one that truly loved me.
For you I'll kneel upon my knee.

IT COULD BE WORSE

Though we think we have the world to fear,
when we lose the one we love so dear.

Though it hurt when we lose our ride,
through public notice it hurts our pride.

Though we lose the most important game,
which hurts our chance to make the hall of fame.

Though no one knew how much it meant,
to lose the race to become president.

Though we sigh when the physician has said,
the conclusion of our lives must be in bed.

The worse my friend is yet to come,
if the end catches you with your work undone.

FRUITS OF THE SPIRIT

Holy Spirit, abide in me, so that I may see:
When hate turns my heart to stone,
and <u>love</u> ceases to be shown.
When my sad countenance,
ill reflects my <u>joyous</u> presence.
When my conflicts persist,
because it's <u>peace</u> that I resist.
<u>Impatience</u> in me,
when helping others so they might see.
When cruel embers burn,
inklings of <u>kind</u>-hearted concerns.
When my bad habits still,
my desire to do <u>goodwill.</u>
When uncertainty is the state,
of my quivering <u>faith.</u>

When I'm too callous to bless,
fellowmen with <u>gentleness.</u>
When my moral compass discloses,
I've lost my <u>self-control.</u>
Holy Spirit, abide in me,
so I might see, Holy.

ON THE VERGE OF HAPPENING

In case you haven't noticed, it's getting rough in this world.
It's getting hard to tell the boys from the girls.
We place our values on material things,
Can someone tell me what all this means.
We give little thought to taking a life,
or living together before husband and wife.
We even preach to the world for personal gain,
swearing we are speaking in God's holy name.
Mother Nature's out of balance again this year,
I can't even tell which season is here.
Note the leaves on the trees, they're beginning to fall;
the calendar says spring but the season is fall.
There's a new war abroad the news media proclaims;
to fight without a purpose is not in God's holy name.
What can this mean, I don't understand,
the sole purpose for God making man.
Soon famine, war and man himself,
will destroy this world; and no man left.

LOOKING AT MYSELF

Looking at the people, and then myself,
I see why people are starving to death.
The role I play in life is common to me.
Life itself is as lonely as can be.
Looking at the people, and then myself,
someone tell me, is there any hope left?
Others in life carry on like me,
snorting that coke, and drinking marijuana tea.
Looking at the people, and then myself,
only God knows when we'll see our death.
Will I learn to love and not to hate?
Will I get right before it's too late?
That's the only way we can save this land.
May I lend the first helping hand?
Looking at the people, and then myself,
I see that helping people is good for your health.
It releases mental tension which relaxes the mind.
I'm glad I looked at myself in time.

I LOVE YOU

It sounds so good coming from my lips.
Just as lyrics from a poet's scrip.
I love you.
I get heart-throbs when I see your face.
My mind transcends to a serene place.
I love you.
Your words inspire a confident mind.
Daily council is of wise design.
I love you.
Your beauty is exposed by day's light.

Your loveliness is aroused by night.
I love you.
I want to kiss your beautiful face.
Your warm body I want to embrace.
I love you.
You have a way of making my day.
I'm so lonely when you go away.
I love you.
It's a sad thought that torments my mind.
When I conceive a time you're not mine.
I love you.
Thinking of you is my lone repose,
Seeing you is a sight to behold.
I love you.
Hoping that time won't cause us to part,
cause you my love are the queen of my heart.
I love you.

I AM MAN

Look at me, I am man.
I reflect the image of those who came before me.
I'm a direct result of the pain, suffering, and dedication
that paved the way for the bright future that awaits me.
I'll charge into the future, illuminated by my past,
hoping to avoid falling into the pits of despair,
by remembering from whence I came.

Look at me. I am man.
But a babe is from where I came to be.
As a babe, I saw the world revolving around me.
I saw good, bad and indifferent.
As a babe, I was persuaded by the force of the hand.

I was nurtured by the comfort of loving arms.
By command I did, by curiosity I did more.
Look at me. I am man.
A direct product of my recent youth.
As a youth, I scurried from command, for I adore me.
I hasten manhood, but man I am not.
For when responsibility arises, don't look at me.
But it is doing my youth, I learn the ways of manhood.

Look at me. I am man.
As a man I stand, evolved from my past.
I ponder the wasted years.
I cherish the years that remain.
Now that I'm man, as a man I'll stand.
As my world revolves, I'll climb aboard.
It is I, who will become a building block
for others to develop their foundation.
It is I, who will offer a helping hand,
guided by arms of love.
It is I, who will challenge the future,
for all it has in store for me.
I am man!

HIGH EXPECTATION

You wake each morning at the break of day,
hoping everything is going your way.
Your eyes view this day for the first time,
Many new things go through you mind.

This is the day you'll reach for the top.
You promise yourself you won't be stopped.

So you think of new ways to earn your gain,
for this is the way you'll earn your fame.

So you rise to the world as a man of art.
You seem happy and gay but really you're not.
You meet each person with a smiling face,
with only 24 hours there is no time to waste.

So you tell everyone of your brand new plan.
How you came to rule and save their land.
No other man has a plan so new.
It must be done when the day is through.

As people become aware of your plan of wit.
You've captured their minds, you must admit.
Now rise to the top and take your stand.
You are unique, strong and fine young man.

Well now my friend what can you say?
Your new plan worked. You rule in a day.
Why aren't things really as they seem?
Awaken my friend, you're lost in a dream.

NEW EDEN

Expelled from providence,
man reaps the consequence.

In New Eden's Garden,
is God's Grace and pardon.

Man now struggles with choice,
of Satan's or God's Voice.

Strolling through the garden,
utmost appetizing.

Man's curiosity thrives,
seeking means to survive.

From a tree, you shall eat,
from which tree, do you seek?

New Eden's Garden yields,
knowledge of Good – Evil.

The sustenance consumed,
seals thy fate, hope or doom.

Good, is so revealing,
evil, so appealing.

Curiosity dictates
as "Shall-Not's" fascinates.

New Eden's residence,
seems void of God's presence.

Temptation ever lures,
my calling now, unsure.

My flesh cheers in delight,
my soul has lost the fight.

Tree of knowledge, do eat.
It yields fruits, bitter, sweet.

The sweet knowledge of good,
inspires a neighborhood.

Yet evil's bitter taste,
can wreck the human race.

Knowledge shall not suffice -
eat thee from the Tree of Life

Seeking knowledge of good,
Abel's fate was assured.

Cain's knowledge of Evil,
conspired acts of ill will.

The vantage point I stand,
evil lurks on all hands.

Who breaks cycles of pain,
so peace abides again?

Seek thee, the Tree of Life,
a balm for pain and strife.

The Tree of Life bridges,
God's wisdom to knowledge.

Find in the Tree of Life,
the Savior, Jesus Christ.

SEARCHING

What type of man am I?
Where does my potential lie?
I don't know the things I should do.
If you could help me, would you?
Which talent I own should I use?
Such a big decision it gets me confused.
What type of image should I display?
It seems so hard to choose the right way.
Can anyone answer the questions I ask?
Before my time on earth has passed?
It seems I hear a voice that says,
think son, your experience will help
you choose the right way.

AT 24

This is a day to remember. A day to rejoice.
For this is the day, I expressed my voice.
It took a blow to the rear to proclaim my life.
Now here I am, wise, intelligent, nice.
It's been a hard climb up to this point,
Obeying the laws of man to stay free of the joint.
Few have understood the road I chose to take.
I follow my own mind and make my own mistakes.
We'll forget the disagreements on this special day.
It's my time to shine, have some birthday cake.
Forget all problems that troubles the mind.
Relax and absorb the rays of golden sunshine.
This day only comes one time a year.
If it didn't come today, I wouldn't be here.

GRADUATION TIME

Standing at my threshold of time,
as if I'm peering from light into darkness.
The secure into insecure.
Peering from the familiar into unfamiliarity.
Currently, I'm familiar
from my getting up to my laying down.
No unfamiliarity.
Yet, one knows from within one's soul,
that one must face the maturation test.
Of one's readiness to leave the nest.
Which way do I go? Or, do I stay?
That's the question of this day.
The question imposes itself upon me.
I did not beckon it, yet, I must answer the call.
Time is of the essence, if I'm prudent.
Less I lose precious time and find myself, lingering in regret.
Lost time is impossible to reclaim.
Through loving nurturing, diverse in nature,
I'm equipped as I stand at the threshold this time.
In retrospect, I swear to be more committed to tasks which I
was uncommitted.
And to stay the course on tasks of which I was committed.
I must use what I've honed, and take the world on.
The time is now to decide.

TRUE CHRISTMAS

Take a look around,
notice the change in the air?
Something strange is happening,
there is joy everywhere.

People hearts are full of love, joy and cheer.
For those who haven't noticed, Christmas time is here.
Christmas is that time of the year,
we show love to those far and near.
As the spirit of Christmas surrounds us again,
Let's spread its love throughout the land.
True Christmas is bread for a starving soul,
or shelter for the lame, lost in the cold.
Let's show love to our fellow man.
May I be the first to lend a helping hand?
True Christmas is blessing those truly in need.
Christmas is made merry through our good deeds.

LOVE AND UNDERSTANDING

Should women or men love or understand?
Answer that question before joining hands.

When you give your mate total love and trust,
what is your base, understanding or lust?

People must remain together today,
before all time on earth has passed away.

Men and women unite until death due part,
with love and trust stored deep in their hearts.

Time causes love to blow away like the sand,
a love can't last if you don't understand.

For understanding on what each should do,
but don't hesitate to say, I love you.

Love keeps understanding pure as the Nun,
moments together will be loving fun.

Love is dependent and can't stand alone,
add understanding and you can't go wrong.

WORK

Work my friend every day,
work my friends you cannot play.
Life is a drag can't you see,
work for the man he'll pay you a fee.
Work each day from 8 to 5,
for hardly enough to stay alive.
Ask for more what does he say,
come back boy on another day.

So, work, work, leave me alone.
Work, work, work, is my brand new song.
Work, work, work, from dust to dawn.
Work, work, work, till the weekend comes.
Work, work, work, oh no, no, no.
Work, work, work, I can't take no more.

I have a wife at home;
She loves to stay on the phone.
I have a kid in school:
Oh man he's cool.
I have a brand new home:
But won't for long.
I had a brand new car:
It was my pride and joy.

So work, work, leave me alone.
Work, work, work, is my brand new song.
Work, work, work, from dust to dawn.
Work, work, work, till the weekend comes.
Work, work, work, oh no, no, no.
Work, work, work, I can't take not more.
.

CAST YOUR LOT

Cast your lot. It's the best shot that you've got.
Un-casted lots, will leave you feeling distraught.
Cast your lot. Give it everything you've got.
Un-casted lots, are as apathetic tots.
Cast your lot. Illuminate dimwit pots.
Un-casted lots, are dim lights for a night-watch.
Cast your lot. Be master over your lot.
Un-casted lots, yield to the wills of despots.
Cast and watch, the impacts of your casted lot.
Un-casted lots, yield you not one single drop.
Cast your lot. Un-casters will stand and watch.
Un-casted lots, are gazed upon as what-nots.
Cast your lot. To meet the needs of have-nots.
Un-casted lots, are over-casted by casted lots.
Casters' nots, overwhelm not casted lots.
So your lot, is chosen by those who cast lots.
A lot casted, is the task you must compass.
Lots un-casted, are as rewards left un-cashed.
Cast your lot. For if you choose to cast not,
un-casted lots, may render you a caste lot.
Cast your lot. It's your unique work of art.
Un-casted lots, are talents that's never been wrought.

NO DOUBT

You are the one, there is no doubt;
you are the one who turns me out.

Each day I look at myself and say,
who is the one that brightens my day?

Who's always there at the right time,
to comfort my tired and weary mind?

Let's face up to it men of the world,
what would we do without a girl?

So whether you confess to it or not,
someone holds the number one spot.

Now laugh at me when I say,
to that special girl that brightens my day.

You are the one, there is no doubt;
you are the one that turns me out.

TO THE LADY I LOVE

Lady love, lady love,
did God send you from above?
Lady love please tell me why,
my heart is open to hear your cry?
You're the one I feel so deep.
You're the dreams and beauty of sleep.
Why do I give my life to you?
Without you, life is sad and blue.

Yes oh yes, I must admit,
my love is long and just won't quit.

THE GOAL AHEAD

There's an important goal in your life,
to which you'll make a great sacrifice.
This is a talent you wish to pursue.
No on owns this talent but you.

Many will say you won't make it to the end.
Those who give confidence are your true friends.
Don't let discouragement cause you to sigh,
Keep a strong mind with your head to the sky.

To achieve a great goal is a hard fight,
so get prepared, don't take it too light.
Condition your body as well as you mind,
you'll reach you goal ahead of time.

If by chance you lose this fight,
remember man rarely knows what's right.
Maybe there's a reason for loosing this time.
You're now ready for the next goal in line.

WHO AM I TO YOU?

Tell me gent, just who am I to you?
A shorty you're just passing through?
Am I the one who you're seeing?
Or you like being seen with me?

Are you playing some game,
when you asked me my name?
You get all in my face,
with your charm and your grace.
And you make me feel good,
like a gentleman should.
And you look so damn sweet,
like the chocolate I eat.
Whenever you're near me,
I feel sheer ecstasy.
But what I really want to know,
is will you let me go,
for someone you really haven't
even gotten to know?
Am I the one who you're seeing?
Or you like being seen with me?

A LOVING PONDER

Sitting on the outside,
thinking about my inside,
wishing you were by my side.

Wondering if this will ever be,
I'll pray and forever wait patiently.

If I could find what's on your mind,
maybe I could make you happy sometime.
If only our minds were of the same kind.

If only I could say the words to make you feel,
that I'm the person that's for real,
my life would be an eternal thrill.

MOM'S APPEAL

While I was still in my formative years.
I decided to wholeheartedly yield.
To my mother's compassionate appeal.
To adopt principles by which to live.

First believe the Word is your saving grace.
Let the Word guide you in this worldly place.
Seek to understand yourself through and through.
Let your own conscience establish self-rule.

Pray to discern the Holy Spirit's call.
Stay true, avoid emotional pitfalls.
Life is as a rising and setting sun.
Rise to overcome, set to life well done.
Thanks Mom!!!

ALL ALONE

Alone. Alone. Never, never, never, alone.
Is what the friendless, hopeless, faithless, bemoans,
when awakens to find, all connections are gone.
Now one finds one's self, virtually all alone.

Being restrained from all means to communicate,
is a most un-welcomed thought to contemplate.
One needs alone-time to refresh a weary mind.
Yet prolonged disconnects harbors lonesome times.

When conflicts arise among one's encounters,
one withdraws to one's emotional shelters.

So the test besets, how to manage alone-time,
so that loneliness is not one's daily pine.
From time to time the thought exacerbates the mind,
for alone-time to be one's daily recline.
When negative encounters doggedly persist,
thoughts of prolonged alone-time can't be resisted.

When the weekly friendship gatherings turns sour,
one tends to find alone-time from those hours.
While alone-time appears to be the perfect mend,
one may've progressed to assess new slates of friends.

When previous endeavors fails to hit the mark,
former brilliant thoughts are deemed not very smart.
A feeling overwhelms that all one's hopes are dashed,
one turns to me, myself and I with dispatch.

When tragedy strikes and takes your precious delight,
and the thought persist to just give up the fight.
After fervent prayers and humble supplication,
leaves a pillar of faith, distraught and shaken.

When there's no one to phone because all friends are gone,
when dashed hopes leaves one in a hopeless syndrome.
When one's faith is too week to chant a worship psalm,
one finds oneself always, always, all alone.

EYES WIDE-SHUT

While perusing around, I found out this most curious thing.
What appeared most obvious, was not all that was to be seen.
The unseen placed limitations, on all of my hopes and dreams.

My eyes were wide-shut, unable to see all that may be seen.

What I saw and what I didn't see, is becoming clear to me.
What I saw, was within the realm of my perception to see.
What I didn't see, was beyond my ability to conceive.
What is clear, my eyes are wide-shut to certain realities.

My eyes are wide-open to see, a people in poverty.
With inflated prices, poor services and exorbitant fees.
My eyes are wide-shut, blind to see, justice in economy.
When shall I see, all people free to attain prosperity?

My eyes are wide-open to see, my health care status is bleak.
I find no good family options affordable to me.
My eyes are wide-shut, blind to see, any good health care relief.
When shall I see, affordable health care for all families?

My eyes are wide-open to see, a neighborhood wretched in
crime.
Having a police force, that never seems to arrive in time.
My eyes are wide-shut, blind to see, crime ceased in streets like
mine.
When shall I see, a time when crime is not the favorite pastime?

My eyes are wide-open to understand, the laws of the land.
And just application, is what the Constitution demands.
My eyes are wide-shut, blind to see, blind justice in penalties.
It appears Lady Justice peeks, when sentencing folks like me.

I can now see, that my eyes are wide-shut, blind to see,
what's what.

UN-BORNE BURDEN BEARER

Who shall bear the burden of cause-reason-purpose?
Who shall bear for us?
Whether selected by tradition, custom, or moral code,
a task awaits us, who shall be the burden bearer?
By reason of tradition, shall it be the elder statesman?
By customary order, shall it be line of succession?
By purpose shall virtue fill the void?
Who shall be the burden bearer? The burden must be borne.
Shall travesty long persist before the bearer arise?
What degree of degradation shall subsist till the bearer is
inspired to bear?
Is the burden bearer conceived by Divine selection?
Or chosen via popular election?
Or by haphazard sets of circumstances?
Who/What/Why, budges the bearer?
Is the bearer known of self, present?
Or later to be inspired, yet unbeknown presently?
Are burdens borne individually, or collectively?
Do we bear ye one another's burdens?
Who shall bear?
What fate awaits the collect when burdens are un-borne by
burden bearers?

THE D.J. OF SOUND

Behold all my friends, please gather around,
And be entertained by the D.J. of Sound.
My music and songs are gifts to you.
They will lift your spirits, you will never be blue.

Step in my parlor of music and here,
all the greatest music, guaranteed to cheer.
Music will electrify a sad soul.
It's the fountain of youth, you'll never grow old.

Open you mind and be music inclined.
Now get you soul in gear it's party time.
If you feel good my friends get up and dance.
It's all up to you how you choose to prance.

There you go my friends, have yourself a ball.
No matter the genre, my sounds are for all.
Clap your hands and stump your feet to the beat.
Enjoy all you can for it's my special treat.

But as time grows near for my sounds to end,
I want all of you to visit my parlor again.
Music is my joy that I spread around,
Compliments to you from the D.J. of Sound.

MOM'S DEDICATION TO HER CHILDREN

Lord, it's not my will, but thy will be done;
I return to thee, each Daughter – each Son.
And with each breath of my live that you give,
I'll be thy example, for each to live.
In a soft austere voice, I'll sow thy truths;
through sober reflections, they'll bear wise fruits.

I will teach them thy word to guide their paths;
as molten vessels, from thy holy cast.
I will inspire, increase of their talents,
to meet the task of each vineyard challenge.
I will promote family unity,
based upon Christian conformity.
I will teach them to sing and praise they name.
Thy goodness, thy mercy, they shall proclaim.
In each community where they might dwell,
they'll live helpful lives, greater than themselves.
And now I establish a Golden Rule;
twelve years only begins their time in school.
My solemn prayer Lord, my plan of hope;
"One Generation Begets the Next Growth".
This plan, children, execute it! I pray;
your true and humble servant, Alice Mae.

DAD'S DEMANDS

A man of meager means, yet abundant dreams.
A man small in size, who thought otherwise.
"Be your own man", to his offspring's he'd command".
"Have many children, own you house, bye land".
He'd further exclaim before taking his noonday nap;
"Never, my child, be anybody's chap".
He taught 14 children to work with their hands;
so we could indeed be our "own man".
"In God" he proclaimed – "Put all your trust".
So he carried us to church in his pick-up truck.
And if you'd listen closely, you will pleasantly hear;
Dad's melodious song and prayer ringing in your ear.

As he leads Taylor's Chapel in devotional song;
"Must Jesus Bear This Cross Alone"?
Your profound words dear dad will always ring clear,
and shall befall on our offspring's ears.
Work with your hands to secure your lot.
Put your trust in God, the best friend you've got.

www.ingramcontent.com/pod-product-compliance
Lightning Source LLC
Chambersburg PA
CBHW071448040426
42445CB00012BA/1486